the flap pamphlet series

Batman's Hill, South Staffs

T0353145

open, read, turn

Batman's Hill, South Staffs

the flap pamphlet series (No. 9)
Printed and Bound in the United Kingdom

Published by the flap series, 2013
the pamphlet series of flipped eye publishing
All Rights Reserved

Cover Design by Petraski
Series Design © flipped eye publishing, 2010

Versions of some of the poems in this pamphlet have appeared
previously in journals and anthologies as follows:
'In Lilac Time' and 'Raymond Earl' in *Critical Survey*.
'Pebble Play' in *The London Magazine*.
'Caroline Caswell' in the anthology *Sylvia Is Missing*, Flarestack Poets.
An earlier version of 'Upper Ballyroe' in *Pennine Platform*.

ISBN-13: 978-1-905233-42-7

LOTTERY FUNDED

Batman's Hill, South Staffs

"Always and everywhere,
this unequal struggle to preserve and remember."
--Ian Jack, The Country Formerly Known As Great Britain
(London: Vintage, 2009)

Michael W. Thomas

Contents | *Batman's Hill, South Staffs*

Dew That Missed Its Morning

1972

I

the place you grew up in
told nothing

roads with their bad meld of borough tar
never ran towards the world's heart

no Delphic shake
from the cricket club wall

though you stared by the hour
a Pied Piper tagalong, sleep-fooled, shoeless

it talked only in pads of moss
readied its long inward topple

but still you go back
get in among the kerbs and porches

lean over the end fence
where that jacaranda was

braced by poles and banisters
more and stouter as summers flew

whose house was it? whose idea
to traffic such beauty

7

jag it down in this unloveliness
lock up its delta spirit to eat itself unseen?

just two poles now
squiring a play-frame

II

up and down you go
round all that old outstation
human feathers caught on hooks
nests of the unflown

still you listen with your skin
for words in those flaking adjacencies

words that knew
how you should have become

which journey-star
should have rounded your eye
when you struck out

they might still be there
swagged on a carriage-lamp's underspike
like dew that missed its morning

III

surely they were there
back in the square heat
of old-money summers
blew across the screaming life
of gangs, jubblies, nettles, diverted mud—
ready to fill you
when you caught breath
cast about for the shapes
to fasten across the next hour
ready to fall against a careless window
come at you in sleep

IV

but no words now
aerial and street-lamp
stop divvying up their horizons
and stare you away

no sound
save the usual scraps
from the engine-hours:
footsteps gaining
on a throb in their owners' heads

somewhere the combustion
of one perch and two magpies

say your words found a readier home
laying back on another kid's river

say you'd have done as well
to climb the sad jacaranda
under a Buzz Aldrin moon
suck down all the sky-going static
get wise any-old-how.

Not that it would have mattered.
Shake your ears clean,
break in on any grove of life:
no-one knows anything

save that time pulls and elbows through
pretending to be a doctor

best go
or it'll have to be the train after next
coming for you in the dark

Outside

1961

Why don't you go outside?
Rain has bagged up its pearl whispers.
Sun jags hard at the patio,
whose slabs my father has left
to find their own horizons.

Stuck in here all day.
Music and cooled shadow,
ways of being loved before I knew it.

You need exercise.
Running with the bones of Robin Hood,
flatting my hand
where ghost trees rattle green memory
around the brute kerbs, the come-lately sodium.

They're all out kicking the ball. Wouldn't hurt.
Voices like drainage,
weasel-feet on municipal remnants.
Friends for as long as a belch
then shin-kicks,
knees on my heart appallingly,
ragged-arsers whose knuckles and shags
will get them no further
than where the bomb
downed the Forgemaster's Arms.

Don't know you're born, you.
Oh, I do, I do,

but I hide the knowing as wafers
in the bureau leaf's running-posts,
down the back of the chair no-one sits on,
where your Zal-shedding arm
never thinks to swing.

You can put that face away.
This is home. Your father's settled.
Except when, as it might be at dusk,
he drives out to those new-build villas,
holds up a fist of money enough
to tease them off their footings--
when he looses spinach-lung breath
hard at their cladding,
magics the notes into another pint,
drinks to the health of a wallowing hippo.

Rain's back. Lucky for you, eh?
Close the door when you go,
slim the gap to nothing
against your floral outrageousness.
Tell the birds they'll taste no sweeter
than the crumbs on the mud-hollow lawn.

Who are you?
Where is your midnight suitcase?
Mine?

[Zal is a household disinfectant that's been on sale forever. It's of the same
vintage as Oxydol washing-powder and Pepsodent toothpaste.]

In Lilac Time

1962

Go down to Kew in lilac time, in lilac time, in lilac time
Go down to Kew in lilac time (it isn't far from London)
--Alfred Noyes, 'The Barrel-Organ'

I remember small rooms
the shin-level gas of dissension

the kitchen chirped once, at Christmas
a red breast beat life through the transom-pane

come Boxing Day the snow was ash
the pantry-mouse flattened its back against another year

on telly people called Askey and Ray
staggered after comedy's clean heels

at school we sang *Rule Britannia*
glowed from it all over playtime like Windscale mistakes

the skin of Assembly visitors
sang its fragrance of Castile

clicked into line
like the sides of an overnight coffin,

voices bittered on early fog, snot a-tumble,
we went down to Kew in lilac time

in lilac time

mom's law came sideways: a maid-of-all-work
flaring a grate inside my face

dad's was the coward's gambit
a secret punch deep in the spine.

At last I shut the gate,
housefronts folded behind my steps

at the crescent's end I died, lived,
broke off a billow of lilac.

Caroline Caswell
1964

Caroline Caswell
was a gap of dawn between two fences.

When her family gathered heads,
bubbled goodbye at their door

hers bobbed highest, a beauty-mask on a stick
a smile that belonged above the coping stones

the cat-curls of Michaelmas fog.
She steadied the streets

taught kerbsides their ps and qs
gentled the crack of stones

against a sleeping window
from some prodigal, keyless in the Saturday dark.

Delinquency pulled its cap flat to its breast
noses, for once, grew a hanky.

Her play walked heel to toe
between etiquette and storm

as a princess might sweep
clear out of some chandeliered whatnot

clip an unpriceable vase with her sleeve
leave it to rock
between smithereens
and foursquare rest

I never knew another kindness
that meant itself so durably, so long.

Scratches appeared on the Caswell door
midnight tiptoe stressed their upturned bin

a stickman devil got in, hairless, yellow
took everything but her smile—

which Offchance gives me
now and then to picture
drops it into my eye
from where chimney cowls
give up against the blue

from where tall trees
buff under that bit of spring
that's so hard to get at.

Pebble Play
1965

Evening. The gathered day
hangs in unfinished spaces:

gateless lawn, a garage door propped
with waste metal

I work to free our house-stone, a pebble
bedded under the call-it-the-dining-room sill

if you get that loose, said dad,
head down, chin breeding chin, we're done for

I take him at his knockabout wisdom,
worry out another planet of sand,

wonder how the sky will treat us
when the pebble's gone, when I kill our life

will the street-corner shitheels
walk straight through where the kitchen lived,

knives of shadow barring oven-pad mom
from the roast she sighs towards?

Will I sleep high in a bucket of air,
spud-guns poxing my bum?

inside, mom and dad laugh at the tv —
a skim of light wakes mirth

at the foot of their gulley. For a giggle's width,
they forget to be what they've become

but it must be done: the pebble
is now a blue half-tuber, shucking vertical ground

heat watches me where it furls like a tramp
in the garage roof's mesmerised ripples.

When the pebble bounces, I'll fly up,
small myself under the heat

till nothing shows, not a tuft,
like on those best nights, Fridays

deep in the eiderdown kingdom;
when school has dropped through another week,

when time skins over the downstairs rages.

Late in the Day

Sunday, 3rd September, 1967

Distance is smoke.
Beyond Great Bridge and Princes End
houses lock together

a model town
seen through a tunnel of doors
folds of last light on its rooftops

the Big Hilly
is now the sleep of dog daisies
summer striking all its canvas.

Dad's dead out on his elbows
my arms are around my knees —
save when the dog
knocks over our silence
stands pot-round and quivery
between one smell-hunt and the next
and his hand or mine
buffs her snout with a sort of love.

Dad and I
in baffled cahoots on open ground
pub suspended,
records and tapes,
the settled trade of indifferences —

cousins at a funeral
photo-prompts to hand

schoolmates colliding
who cleared throats for the next word
forty years ago.

Two old fellers
come down the Hilly
trouser-hitching
bellows to an argument
that might have got going
when that uppity bit of paper
slapped Chamberlain in the face:

And the day you turn round—
Don't start all that again—
Listen, you, listen! The day you turn round—
Shut your hole, can't be doing—
Day you turn round and you say to me . . .

their mufflers, caps, incontinent grudge
drop below the shoulder of the hill

with a back-swinging chuckle
Dad throws their words up and over the heavens
makes Venus flare
like a goosed baroness

the dog gets in on it
ferrying a lick from his laughter to mine.

Lights are buttoned over Great Bridge,
Princes End, Hoyt, the Lost City

what time d'you call this?
is by now trailing mom like a Bisto-waft
from door to drive to window.

Upper Ballyroe, Kilfinnane

1968, the Uncle's farm

We stand and watch the rain.
The sloping field
strikes loose its waters
rides them down
to pools of mahogany gumbo.

The hayricks are what's left
when mountains unbuckle their splendours
fall by fall. Their crowns cave and suck.
Chemistry happens. The rotten stem
swaddles the firm.

One of us is leant against a tree,
swelling its black scars
with crooked breath, head stuck
in last night's fuddle.
His free hand wags at his hip,
—a cigarette strung on its fingers.

Someone forecasts: brighter than scrubbed beans
come teatime. Then we'll get on.
Fecksakes, the cig flares back at him,
it's torrents now, well into the boozing hour
and down to the heel of tomorrow besides.
We'll see the summer out forking blancmange,
and where were the bloody tarps?

The tarps are asleep,
interfolded like sofa cats
in the barn we walked past hours ago,
swatting off the sun . . .

. . . which someone else swears he's glimpsed,
just, way and gone over the field:
a finger of it laid underside
the gapping wounds of cloud.
Ah, he insists, it'll turn for us now.

But it has business
with cliffs and trawling-roads.
It slithers off (*Fecksakes*)--another kind of cat,
squeezing up space for itself
under the sag of a dresser,
or with the last of retreat up its tail
as a window unratchets and slams.

Raymond Earl
1969

Raymond Earl didn't have a single doorknob
in all his head

took a *Shut* sign to the world
save when it fed and pillowed him

or dug about for a joke he might rattle to,
a face he might hail through his deepwater light

but give him a ball and he could vapourize
the dictates of Hannibal. Thigh to foot

he drove without a car
wore down a realm of sixpences

with brake and spin. Up close,
skidding, despairing of a tackle,

you heard him prove the nothingness of words
bump noise far to the back of his throat

show that language only worked
when poured south to the engine muscles

then he was gone, leaving you
in your man-trap of turf

with a ghost on your right foot
re-tingling the jump of the ball.

He had a trial for Wolves.
Didn't fancy. Early mornings. No chips.

Last time I saw him was in the wounded hollows
of the district park

hup-hupping a World Cup '66 ball—
Bobby Moore's name, Nobby's, Geoff's and Jack's

hanging like suns the sky was made for,
petitioning the hem of an archangel's gown

with mud and genius

A Prince in August

Trevor Anglin,1970

A boy walks into a throw of sun

fifty yards ago
he slid out of a fog-stopped room—

ashtray mom with her new sprout
of woe, manning all trajectories

tile-cat sis, brother struck down
in a castor-less chair, watching

how the walls meet—the odd word
strung from the roof of his head

not enough to pray back the telly.

A mile on and the boy
will loaf against the slow climb of stars

just off the pub's boundary
press a shoulder of underpacked bone

to a pole with a recipe for voltage
offer the whites of his baseball boots

for the sinking world to admire
wink at girls who don't come his way

channel cop show threats at some foe
who faces him invisibly down

arms a shade clear of his body
from the Bermuda of nettles across the road

if his uncle's inside, if he happens out
to flourish a piss by the tar-blocks

the boy might get a half or its froth
or anyway a whiff of the hand

that mountaineered under the barmaid's apron
otherwise it's home

his body peeling shadows hardly fatter
than the pallet-yard rails.

But for this moment the sun has him
where it lies like the slops of Olympus

between the shop end and a mews of lock-ups
it flushes gold his penny-round collar

arrays his jacket for Assembly Rooms
the self-delighting languor of Regency sport

invites his eyes to see
how he is ruffed and prinked for Samarkand

should go there now by boat-train
by moon-fathomed roads

but they fall cold and insensible
like his dad's goodbye

remember just in time to check
the last house on the right
where that mental dog is.

Thin Places

Llan, Shropshire, Autumn 1971

*For George MacLeod, founder of the Iona Community after the
First World War, a thin place was one where the gap between
heaven and earth hardly exists.*

At Clunton Coppice I coughed once, twice
and troubled nothing

twigs were fishing the wind already
a smudge on the uplands howled anyway

down in Clunbury
a pub had thrown its pork-and-spillage arms about my dad

the day would fall off its meridian
taking down his songs and money

I'd drive. Fourth lesson
gears as far beyond my robotics as ever

from here to home, the scarps and passes:
Craven Arms, Hurst Hill, Woodsetton
laying their ice against a vulture sky.

Made up of depots and rolling-yards
when did I last walk
outside a generated sun?

things in their quiet
got between me and my feet

goats went dainty as assassins
a horse rested its fear

on a staple-matted post, so I was inches
from a wet eye, a hulking radiance

its mouth worked like a madman's
whose tears go down the wrong way

a black quilt threw itself
across the top of the clouds

broke into a hundred shapes
of wooded preening

pheasants wallowed into their height
with the prang of Edwardian gadgetry

in one field
the afternoon roosted on a ticklish pond

another sat its frosts in a ring
like a ruckle-top pie

belly-up, a ewe cycled her forelegs
watched a pony
headless in the last fat barrows of green.

A signpost
where high road sighed into low —

broken fingers
two directions long seeded under the land
one way, my dad
distressing moonlight and roses

the other, nothing
everything.

The air thinned about my irresolution
call it the company of heaven I heard

the crump of wings
infinite through north gulley, south brake

a song without the bruise of meaning
out and away over all the wired hills

call it the year's last cluster-flies I saw
threading the road's emptiness
while my pocket-hand gripped dad's keys

dancing as skeins of prayer
while my hand loosened

dancing as crosses
while my foot beat off sudden snow

and pounding, braced, I walked forward
walked through

resolved to give my rearing past
the slip.

Decree Nisi
1971

These days I sleep. You may have watched my hand
reach for the same tin as yours on a shelf.
What can I do but apologise for
my fingers' barging grasp, my fencing arm?
We no longer speak.

And yet I am much about. My body
assembles life enough to hang in step
down streets in their mid-morning idleness,
can thread steam over lightless dawn for drinks
which throat and cock in phase will attend to
while I scull through my otherwheres.

Of course there are two faces leaning in
like ignorance at windows when you choose
to eat alone. I hugely remember:
they forwarded their world to me, they set
their little angers dancing in my eyes.
Their hands loved their hips, they wore the spent light
of vestibules, shrank and wizened inside
the gospels of themselves.

It's alright. What leans in loses footing.
Each day they lie nearer forest than plain.
Some tomorrow will come with lock and wire

and I'll walk as before

my shadow in my pocket
gaze at posters for amazements
gone or never held
find sun-stones in evening hedges
watch a single swan
split the canal into fool's crystals

I'll be again the fullness of white weather
on my land.
.